Genre Drama

Essential Question
How do you decide what is important?

Midas
and the
Donkey Ears

— **A Play** —

retold by Elizabeth Brereton
illustrated by Clare Caddy

Midas and the Donkey Ears

Characters

Townsperson
Pan
King Midas
Apollo
Barber
Mother Earth

Props Needed

chair
crown
mirror
winner's wreath
donkey ears
scissors

The Music Contest

King Midas sits on his throne, facing the audience. He is wearing a crown. Pan and Apollo stand at either side of him. Townsperson enters, stage right, and faces the crowd.

TOWNSPERSON: In Ancient Greece, there was once a vain and foolish king, who was obsessed with wealth. One day, two gods asked this king to judge a singing contest between them. This is how our story begins…

(Townsperson exits, stage right.)

PAN: (*smiling*) My dear friend, King Midas. I have prepared a song just for you.

KING MIDAS: Oh, Pan, I always love to hear you sing. I know you will do well in this contest.

APOLLO: (*upset*) Perhaps you should wait to hear us both before you decide the winner, King Midas. I, too, possess a beautiful voice.

KING MIDAS: Oh, yes—of course, Apollo. Please begin.

(*Apollo sings. King Midas takes little notice of him. Instead, he admires himself in a mirror.*)

KING MIDAS: The song was pleasing, Apollo. But the tone and pitch were not as good as I would have expected. Let us hear the wonderful Pan sing.

(*Pan sings. King Midas listens enthusiastically.*)

KING MIDAS: (*jumping up from his throne, clapping*) Beautiful! Marvelous! Wonderful! I think we have a clear winner here. Yes, yes, Pan has won the music contest! He gets the reward. Well done, Pan!

(*King Midas awards Pan the winner's wreath. Pan exits, grinning, stage right.*)

APOLLO: That was unfair, King Midas. My voice is far superior to Pan's, yet you chose him to be the winner. Perhaps there is something wrong with your ears. (*rubs his chin*) In fact, I think your ears must be too small to hear properly. I will give you donkey ears!

(*King Midas looks alarmed. He gasps and takes off his crown, revealing donkey ears. He screams and runs off, stage left. Apollo laughs and exits, stage right.*)

STOP AND CHECK

Who won the singing competition?
Why did he win?

Scene Two

A New Hairstyle

Mother Earth enters, sits on the floor, stage right, and freezes.

King Midas, wearing his crown, enters, stage left, and sits in the barber's chair.

Barber enters, stage left, and stands behind King Midas, holding a pair of scissors.

KING MIDAS: Barber, something terrible has happened. If I show you my secret, will you promise to keep it?

BARBER: Of course, Your Majesty. I promise.

(King Midas removes the crown, revealing his donkey ears. Barber gasps.)

KING MIDAS: No one must know of this. Who would obey me if they knew that I have donkey ears?

BARBER: Yes, yes. No one must find out. But can you not keep them covered with your crown?

KING MIDAS: No, that will not work. I cannot wear my crown every minute of every day. It is necessary for you to give me a new hairstyle that will hide these ears. Now, get to work!

(*Barber cuts and combs the king's hair. Finally, the ears are hidden. The king looks at himself this way and that in the mirror.*)

KING MIDAS: That's better. Now I can go out in public again.

(King Midas pays Barber and exits, stage right. Barber paces the stage.)

BARBER: Oh, what a secret! I cannot keep it to myself! But I promised not to tell anybody. What should I do? I could whisper it to Mother Earth. Yes, I will dig a hole in the ground and tell only Mother Earth.

Barber leaves his shop and digs a hole outside. Mother Earth's circled arms form the hole. He kneels by it.

BARBER: (*whispering into the hole*) King Midas has donkey ears! King Midas has donkey ears!

(*Mother Earth giggles and leans closer to hear.*)

BARBER: King Midas has donkey ears! King Midas has donkey ears! (*standing*) There! Now I feel better!

(*Barber exits, stage right. Mother Earth giggles and exits, stage left.*)

STOP AND CHECK

Why did King Midas want a new hairstyle?

Scene Three

The Secret Is Out!

King Midas, Pan, Townsperson, Barber, and Apollo enter, stage right. The king sits on his throne. Mother Earth enters, stage left, and hides. She begins to make the sound of a light breeze.

TOWNSPERSON: Look at his hair! Why did he want it cut like that?

BARBER: I can't say.

MOTHER EARTH: (*whispering*) King Midas has donkey ears!

TOWNSPERSON: (*looking around*) What's that?

BARBER: I think it was the wind.

MOTHER EARTH: (*louder*) King Midas has donkey ears!

TOWNSPERSON: That wasn't just the wind. That was Mother Earth speaking. I can almost hear what she is saying.

MOTHER EARTH: (*even louder*) King Midas has donkey ears!

TOWNSPERSON: (*very loudly*) Really? King Midas has donkey ears!

(*King Midas looks up in anguish.*)

PAN: Is this true, King Midas? Do you have donkey ears?

KING MIDAS: (*taking off his crown*) Yes, it's true. Apollo gave me donkey ears, and now look at me. It is so unfair!

APOLLO: King Midas, I gave you donkey ears because you were not a fair judge. But I see that you have not learned your lesson. Perhaps you should go and live with the donkeys!

(*Everyone laughs.*)

(King Midas exits, stage left. Apollo, Pan, Barber, and Mother Earth exit, stage right. Townsperson faces the audience.)

TOWNSPERSON: From then on, every time the wind blew, Mother Earth whispered King Midas's secret. The foolish king could not stand people making fun of him. Some say that King Midas gave up his crown and his treasure and hid from people's laughter. Others say that King Midas kept his crown and became a different kind of king—a king of the donkeys! Hee-haw!

STOP AND CHECK

How did everyone find out about the king's donkey ears?

Respond to Reading

Summarize

Use details from the story to summarize *Midas and the Donkey Ears*. Your chart may help you.

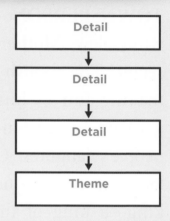

Text Evidence

1. How do you know that *Midas and the Donkey Ears* is a play and a myth? GENRE

2. What is the main message of this story? Find an example in the text. THEME

3. *Unfair* means the opposite of *fair*. Therefore, *fair* is the root word. Choose another word in the text, and tell its root. ROOT WORDS

4. What lesson was *Midas and the Donkey Ears* intended to teach? WRITE ABOUT READING

Compare Texts
Read about a person who learns a lesson.

It's Party Time!

Jake spotted his best friend sitting with the rest of their basketball team. He walked over.

"So, are we all invited to your birthday party?" asked Matt as Jake sat down.

"Of course!" Jake replied. "I want the whole team there."

"Go Tigers!" Simon yelled.

"I've also invited Liam," said Jake.

"Who's Liam?" Simon asked.

"Jake's neighbor," Matt said, rolling his eyes.

"Liam is my friend. He goes to school at Western," Jake said.

"Whatever. He's not on the team, so he shouldn't come," Matt said.

After school that day, Jake met Liam
at their usual spot so they could walk
home together.

"Are you looking forward to your party?"
Liam asked as they walked home.

Jake shrugged his shoulders and didn't
reply. He was thinking about what Matt
had said.

"Look at this," Liam said. He pulled a soccer
ball out of his gym bag and bounced it from
one foot to the other.

"Cool!" said Jake. "May I try?"

Jake tried the balancing trick, but the ball
fell off his foot right away. They laughed.

"I guess I need more practice," Jake said.

"Why don't you
borrow my ball
for a while?"
Liam suggested.

Jake smiled at
Liam. He was a good
friend. "Thanks, Liam.
See you at my party."

There was still half an hour before the party was due to end, and everyone looked bored.

"Where's your friend?" Matt asked.

Jake couldn't see Liam. He sighed. The other guys had ignored Liam. Just then, he saw Liam kicking his soccer ball in the yard.

"Come and play!" Liam called out.

Jake raced outside. One by one, the others drifted out, too. Soon they were all having fun.

"Awesome party, Jake," said Liam later.

"Yeah, it was. Thanks to you!" Jake said.

Make Connections

How did Liam's friendship teach Jake something important? ESSENTIAL QUESTION

How are Midas in *Midas and the Donkey Ears* and Matt in *It's Party Time!* both unfair to somebody else? TEXT TO TEXT

Focus on Genre

Plays Plays are written to be performed in front of an audience. The people who perform in a play are called actors. Stage directions describe what the actors do. Props, such as the donkey ears and the crown in *Midas and the Donkey Ears*, help the story to come alive. Plays have scenes instead of chapters.

Read and Find In *Midas and the Donkey Ears*, the names of the characters are written in upper case and bold. A colon separates the name of the character from the words that the character will speak. The stage directions are written in italics. These directions tell the actors what to do.

Your Turn

Imagine what happened to Midas when he left his castle. Maybe he asked the donkeys if he could join them. Maybe he went to live in another place. Write another scene for *Midas and the Donkey Ears* telling what happened to Midas. Remember to use text features to show which character is speaking and what the character is saying and doing.